Mary will bring forth a Son, and you shall call his name Jesus,
for he will save his people from their sins. Matthew 1:21

Mary will bring _ _ _ _ _ a Son, and you shall call his name
_ _ _ _ _, for he will save his _ _ _ _ _ _ from their _ _ _ _.
Matthew 1:21

A voice came from heaven saying, 'This is my beloved Son in whom I am well pleased.' Matthew 3:17

A _ _ _ _ _ _ came from _ _ _ _ _ _ _ saying, 'This is my
_ _ _ _ _ _ _ _ Son in whom I am well pleased.' Matthew 3:17

Jesus began to preach and to say, 'Repent, for the kingdom of heaven is at hand.' Matthew 4:17

Jesus began to _ _ _ _ _ _ and to say, '_ _ _ _ _ _, for the
_ _ _ _ _ _ _ of heaven is at hand.' Matthew 4:17

I say to you, love your enemies, bless those who curse you, do good to those who hate you. Matthew 5:44

I say to you, love your _ _ _ _ _ _ _, bless those who
_ _ _ _ _ you, do good to those who _ _ _ _ you.
Matthew 5:44

Lay up for yourselves treasures in heaven, where neither moth nor rust destroys. Matthew 6:20

Lay up for yourselves _ _ _ _ _ _ _ _ _ _ in heaven, where _ _ _ _ _ _ _ moth nor _ _ _ _ destroys. Matthew 6:20

Ask and it shall be given to you; seek and you will find; knock and it will be opened to you. Matthew 7:7

_ _ _ and it shall be _ _ _ _ _ to you; _ _ _ _ and you will find; _ _ _ _ _ and it will be opened to you. Matthew 7:7

Whoever does the will of my Father in heaven is my brother
and sister and mother. Matthew 12:50

_ _ _ _ _ _ _ does the will of my _ _ _ _ _ _ in heaven is my
brother and _ _ _ _ _ _ and mother. Matthew 12:50

Jesus spoke to them in parables saying, 'Behold, a sower went out to sow.'
Matthew 13:3

Jesus spoke to them in _ _ _ _ _ _ _ _ saying, ' _ _ _ _ _ _,
a _ _ _ _ _ went out to sow.' Matthew 13:3

When Jesus saw the crowd, he was moved with compassion for them and healed their sick. Matthew 14:14

When _ _ _ _ _ saw the crowd, he was _ _ _ _ _ _ with compassion for them and _ _ _ _ _ _ their sick.
Matthew 14:14

Unless you are converted and become as little children, you will by no means enter the kingdom of heaven. Matthew 18:3

Unless you are _ _ _ _ _ _ _ _ _ and become as little
_ _ _ _ _ _ _ _ _, you will by no means enter the _ _ _ _ _ _ _
of heaven. Matthew 18:3

Jesus said, 'Let the little children come to me, and do not forbid them, for of such is the kingdom of heaven.' Matthew 19:14

Jesus said, 'Let the _ _ _ _ _ _ children come to me, and do not _ _ _ _ _ _ them, for of such is the kingdom of _ _ _ _ _ _.' Matthew 19:14

Jesus came to Gethsemane and said to his disciples, 'Sit here while I go and pray over there.' Matthew 26:36

Jesus came to _ _ _ _ _ _ _ _ _ _ _ and said to his
_ _ _ _ _ _ _ _ _, 'Sit here while I go and _ _ _ _
over there.' Matthew 26:36

When the centurion and those with him ... saw the earthquake and the things that had happened ... they said 'Truly this was the Son of God.'
Matthew 27:54

When the _ _ _ _ _ _ _ _ _ and those with him ... saw the _ _ _ _ _ _ _ _ _ _ and the things that had happened ... they said '_ _ _ _ _ this was the Son of God.' Matthew 27:54

The angel answered ... 'He is not here; for he is risen.' Matthew 28:6

The _ _ _ _ _ answered ... 'He is not _ _ _ _ ;
for he is _ _ _ _ _.' Matthew 28:6

I am with you always, even to the end of the age. Matthew 28:20

I am with you _ _ _ _ _ _, even to the end of the _ _ _.
Matthew 28:20

Ask the Lord of the harvest, therefore, to send out workers
into his harvest field. Matthew 9:38

Ask the _ _ _ _ of the harvest, therefore, to send out
_ _ _ _ _ _ _ into his _ _ _ _ _ _ _ field. Matthew 9:38